WORLDLY THINGS

WORLDLY THINGS
MICHAEL KLEBER-DIGGS

MAX RITVO POETRY PRIZE | SELECTED BY HENRI COLE

MILKWEED EDITIONS

Published 2021 by Milkweed Editions
Printed in Canada
Cover design by Mary Austin Speaker
Cover photograph by Wing Young Huie
21 22 23 24 25   5 4 3 2 1
First Edition

Milkweed Editions, an independent nonprofit publisher, gratefully acknowledges sustaining support from our Board of Directors; the Alan B. Slifka Foundation and its president, Riva Ariella Ritvo-Slifka; the Amazon Literary Partnership; the Ballard Spahr Foundation; *Copper Nickel*; the McKnight Foundation; the National Endowment for the Arts; the National Poetry Series; the Target Foundation; and other generous contributions from foundations, corporations, and individuals. Also, this activity is made possible by the voters of Minnesota through a Minnesota State Arts Board Operating Support grant, thanks to a legislative appropriation from the arts and cultural heritage fund. For a full listing of Milkweed Editions supporters, please visit milkweed.org.

Library of Congress Cataloging-in-Publication Data

Names: Kleber-Diggs, Michael, author.
Title: Worldly things / poems by Michael Kleber-Diggs.
Description: First edition. | Minneapolis, Minnesota : Milkweed Editions, 2021. | Summary: "Worldly Things is the 2020 winner of the Max Ritvo Poetry Prize, selected by Henri Cole"-- Provided by publisher.
Identifiers: LCCN 2020054861 (print) | LCCN 2020054862 (ebook) | ISBN 9781571315168 (hardback) | ISBN 9781571317636 (ebook)
Subjects: LCGFT: Poetry.
Classification: LCC PS3611.L44236 W67 2021 (print) | LCC PS3611.L44236 (ebook) | DDC 811/.6--dc23
LC record available at https://lccn.loc.gov/2020054861
LC ebook record available at https://lccn.loc.gov/2020054862

Milkweed Editions is committed to ecological stewardship. We strive to align our book production practices with this principle, and to reduce the impact of our operations in the environment. We are a member of the Green Press Initiative, a nonprofit coalition of publishers, manufacturers, and authors working to protect the world's endangered forests and conserve natural resources. *Worldly Things* was printed on acid-free 100% postconsumer-waste paper by Friesens Corporation.

for my mother Lequetta,
my wife Karen,
my daughter Elinor,
my brother Martin,
& my mentor Juliet

CONTENTS

One

Two

Three

Exhaust the little moment. Soon it dies.
And be it gash or gold it will not come
Again in this identical disguise.

—GWENDOLYN BROOKS

ONE

END OF CLASS

Black boy in the backseat of a cop car
across the street from my daughter's jr. high,

hands cuffed behind his back: hard to see
him like that. It's an attractive afternoon

here among the thriving—snow glistening, sun
descending on the best block in the city. I have

friends who live nearby so I'm sure I fit right
in with the rich folks and professors. But him?

He's barely surviving the day, and looks at me
from his sick situation as if to say: *Fuck your pity!*

Canary in a coalmine, negro in the pipeline,
his life is full of cages. He's in the wrong

system too soon—tragedies intertwining.
In the rearview mirror, I meet my own

targeted skin and sigh. I'm angry, chagrined.
Until my sweet kid climbs in next to me,

as happy as she can be before I point to
the scene to ask what the boy did. *Oh, Felix?*

He's pretty cool. Sometimes he can be mean.
I think he's on probation. That's all she has to say.

I pat her arm, start the car, and then we drive
away. Our hardy home is not that far from here.

SOURCE OF MY CONFIDENCE

Vast sky, sky blue. Placid dry ocean
sky. I count four cirrus clouds.
I open every window I have
wide. Spring air races through rooms:
a joyous child. My neighbor battens
down for an imminent storm.
She winds in her awnings. She won't
water her garden. This continues
for more than a week. Every day
we have the same conversation.

Get ready, she says,
I feel it in my bones.
I usually respond with mathematics.
They don't know, she says, *they don't
know*. Night allows me
the smallest violence. I fill
a watering can near to overflowing.
I stand in her dark yard and minister
to her flowers. A gentle wind
surrounds me like a robe.

THE AMERICAN VARIETY

In the modern version, the remix, reboot,
retelling, Echo becomes an Alabama mama

so obsessed with Narcissus that she wants him
to love her baby (which, of course, he cannot).

This time Narcissus is no Adonis. In fact, he's
grotesque. He has vile teeth and a nasty mouth.

Tangerine flesh. His hair is tragicomedy, but he's
rich in a land where wealth makes winners, and

winners can't lose. This is the American way—
screen tested in Encino for maximum play in

Tuscaloosa, and this is not a cautionary tale. This
story is not meant to bring you down; it's meant

to lift you up. It's meant to make you feel great
again. So, Narcissus never stops by a river, never

starves. He thrives. He grows bigger and bigger
but never explodes. Instead, he's fed by every

storefront he passes, every shimmery reflection
of himself seen in the eyes of every Echo.

His legend blooms and blossoms until, eventually,
he becomes a popular flower—easy to plant,

impossible to kill, invasive, perennial.

I LOVE MY NEIGHBORS AS I LOVE MYSELF

I drive around admonishing strangers.
Hurry up! I tell them. Or, *Wear a helmet!*
Kids needing parental guidance get it from me.
Teens in black clothes at midnight, sensed
but not seen like owls, receive my words as care.
When I spy an elderly woman with her coat worn loose,
I don't hesitate to yell: *Button up!* I want the best
for her. I learned of love in harsh commands, curt
rebukes and tired, ravenous hands. The rearview
holds ancestral eyes, ravaged, not mine; the hard
hand sending the window down isn't mine—it's
mine. Love is history plus desire. Love is dominion.
It is supposed to attack you. When you send it out,
it stings you back like a slap of cold air.
Sometimes it arrives in the form of a man,
driving away, shouting.

AFTER YOU LEFT

the weight of your absence
became a black hole revolving
around my memory of you—itself
a black hole. Wavelets wrinkled
the sheer sheet of space and time.
Father, the loss of you is a planet
orbiting what might have been.
I cannot say if the emptiness is
a grand celestial body or a vacuum
so complete nothing can escape. I know
these forces have mass and motion
that bends, calls in, ripples fabric—
distorts the pace of light
for a billion years.

SUPERMAN AND MY BROTHER, SPIDERMAN AND ME

My brother and I were born to educated, middle-class parents
eleven days after Martin Luther King's assassination.

Our home aspired to non-violence—no gun culture, no
guns. Even then, folks knew black boys in a white city needed

more than their parent's desire to stay safe; they understood
about misunderstandings. Even then, black boys were shot

in parks playing games children play. So, when we turned
eight, instead of squirt guns, we got puffy superhero heads

that sprayed water from their mouths when we pulled the trigger.
We delighted in comic-book legends spitting on our friends

at our behest. It was white boys on the block with their pistols
and revolvers that always shot harder and farther,

against Superman and my brother, Spiderman and me.
We gave as good as we got until we were exhausted.

1976, the bicentennial year—summer suggested
it would never end, but autumn always comes.

One month before our birthday, our father was shot
and killed in his office. He was a dentist. I tell you that

for a reason. I use *educated* and *middle-class* for a reason.
I don't want you to think our Dad had it coming. I want

you to focus on something else—our parents' designs
were undone anyway; there is no sanctuary in the theater.

Lost for months in our bedroom, our desperate island,
we began to confront a loss that reveals itself still, spent

our allowance on comic books, dreamed of rough places
made plain, tried to hew hope from a mountain of despair.

AFTER THEY LEFT

we policed ourselves, restored our spirits
in quiet tasks until the earth ran red
with iron and sweat. We called old seeds
from the cavernous cold to rejoin them
with the heartsick soil, then tended our crops
by hand. Every day everyone bent down
on knees to pull the weeds away.
Pests took their part but left plenty.
Each harvest, the village gathered together.
To each a share. For all it had suffered
our body stayed whole. Trauma dissipated.
Where our wounds were acute, we applied
more salve, calling our injured closer in, as we
sang to them and give them more fruit.

A SIMPLE QUESTION

I have one question: I say to the therapist. She is black
like me, blacker maybe. Her hair is reddish or auburn,

somewhere in that range. A textured jacket and pencil
skirt frame her well. I don't think about her neckline.

She is maternal to some, I suppose. I like her eyewear—full
of complications she doesn't seem to care about, suggesting

a vanity I'd likely find useful if I intended to stay past
this one visit. Her lips are dusty, dry. Her nose is familiar

and lovely. There is a couch here—an actual couch.
I'm distracted by her silence, by a mahogany bookcase

with three shelves off to the side, decorated with self-help
books written by people who list degrees after their names.

One asks *Whatcha Gonna Do with that Duck?* Another is
The Psychedelic Explorer's Guide. I get the game now—

she isn't going to ask about my parents or my childhood.
She's not going to say anything until I do. The sun is

low in the sky—shoots through her spotty windows
like a searchlight; it splits us into separate shadows.

I don't lie on the couch because that feels weird, typical.
On a crowded shelf, there's a book called *Mindsight.*

Somewhere in the room a clock lurches and stops, lurches
and stops. *Why do I never wake up laughing?* I ask her.

She looks at me and does not stop looking at me. I am
meant to feel awkward in this lingering—self-conscious,

so I don't. I won't. No matter what, I will not speak next.
There is a tiny tape recorder on her desk, but I can tell

it isn't on. She scribbles a sentence, maybe two. For some
reason, she does not lick her lips. She raises her head, lifts

her soft chin in appraisal of me, sets the paper down, pen.
I notice fingerprints on her lenses. She will never see me.

SEISMIC ACTIVITIES

My father died at the edge of spring

                              My daughter was born   as summer waned

unexpected like an earthquake

                              There is no way to prepare   for rapture

or rupturing   a disruption when everything

                              when what you know   and who you are

becomes something else   is subsumed

                              is ravaged by flame then remade

I loved my father but he frightened me

                              I recall being invaded by fear

Once, he sent rage like fire into my face

                              I reeled   staggered and dizzy   burning nerves

I had a hard time keeping my feet on the ground

                              I tried to figure out   what I'd done to deserve

total torture   I wanted my father to be

                              a blessing   a miracle for me   something

more than my tormentor   and he was

                         beautiful too   *heartbreakingly beautiful*

I remember hitting baseballs one autumn

                                I probably imagined innocence   *a shield*

I was a child   we were in our backyard

                not much later I'd set my girl down   *mean, my rage*

a ball I threw—dad put a hurtin' on it

                        a sphere   *shaped like a fist*   *so fast*

with such velocity everything froze

                        I jerked back from it instinctively

a bullet, a bullet, a bullet, a bullet

                   You never forget the shape of   *a shocked mouth*

all around us grass was browned

              wilted   *spoiled*   *I can pinpoint the moment*

the earth shook and came apart

                 the house moved   *my mirror fell and shattered*

I learned death travels at 2500 feet per second

I saw yesterdays and tomorrows   I found out

(those who love us can destroy us)

                (we can destroy those we love   Listen)

the ball cleared the yard   and entered the woods

               no one can hurt like those   who've been hurt

      like my father

                         no one can hurt like me

SUSTENANCE

In pre-dawn dark, I bring pot down
to stove, fire. The news, the mail
surround, threaten, overwhelm. I measure
milk and add it. I won't watch it to a boil.
Patter and pop will call—then oats,
a pinch of salt, once golden fields unfolding
in an old ceramic bowl—to this, my own
base hunger for our daily bread
and my gray ration.

ADAPTATION

Nothing nearby for me to lean on. Nowhere
to rest. A pebble underfoot has grown insistent,
a burdensome tooth. I've had to master
balance. These years, this life have made
of me a common ostrich.
I tuck up a leg, remove my shoe,
release the round stone, watch it bounce
away. I can't fly anymore, but I'm
made to run. I am faster than you
might allow for a creature standing still
like this. Years and
life—I've had to be.

ODE TO MY MOTHER'S FACE

Crowned by carob and silver down, lovely across
her Oklahoma earthen glow, my mother's face is
an ovate frame with apostrophe eyebrows possessing
the massive planets of her eyes. I love her countenance
captured in a photo from fifty years ago, before her lover
was killed and not replaced, before the joys and blood
of motherhood—a powdery base against her sharp white
uniform, a tidy nurse's cap resting comfortably on her
nest of ideas, her graduate's smile, her tirelessness. But not
like I love her face at eighty: her ears unchanged in size,
the knot she owns above her heavy glasses, sad growths
crowding her eyes, deep folds arching away from her
widening nose, around her skeptical mouth like parentheses
staging the lush curtains of her lips, the ones letting you have
just enough show to realize you're missing something.
My mother is the lone freckle on her right cheek, put in place
by providence. A period wanting the next sentence.

IN CONVENIENCE

She never called it industry, grandmother didn't,
but everything served a particular purpose.

Consider dinner: probably chicken and green beans
from her garden, a tiny butterhead lettuce salad

with tomatoes, cucumbers, and yellow onions,
warm bread from grain she grew then ground herself,

preserves from some other season fetched up
from the cellar. She would have chosen a chicken

earlier in the day, chased it down, undressed it
then dressed it, put bones to boil for stock,

used feathers to line the coop, sent beak and claws
and everything else not needed out to field—

if not for carrion exactly, useful in some other way.
I study her in the small kitchen we had at our farmhouse

in Oklahoma, standing resolutely in old resoled shoes,
wearing a dress she'd sewn from a Simplicity pattern—

the source of her apron, too. I watch her setting aside
the gizzard and guts, then turn to start a cake.

I was never really there, even when I was.
I would have been outside picking up rocks

or fishing at the pond—so alive. By my time
we were well into the appliance age, frozen things

assembled and shipped from factories far away,
grabbed at the grocery, stored in our basement freezer—

not better, no one felt that way, but easier, freeing up
time for other pursuits. Women could work

to support the war, then leisure might make our lives
richer—we might go to sock hops, take up tennis,

make art. Behind my house today, a blue bin
holds bottles, newspapers, plastics, foils. A black bin

holds our trash—wrappers mostly. I put a banana
peel from Guatemala into a small green bin with

all the food we didn't eat.

GLORIA MUNDI

Come to my funeral dressed as you
would for an autumn walk in the woods.

Arrive on your schedule; I give you permission
to be late, even without good cause.

If my day arrives when you had other plans, please
proceed with them instead. Celebrate me

there—keep dancing. Tend your gardens. Live
well. Don't stop. Think of me forever assigned

to a period, a place, a people. Remember me
in stories—not the first time we met, not the last,

a time in between. Our moment here is small.
I am too—a worldly thing among worldly things—

one part per seven billion. Make me smaller still.
Repurpose my body. Mix me with soil and seed,

compost for a sapling. Make my remains useful,
wondrous. Let me bloom and recede, grow

and decay, let me be lovely yet
temporal, like memories, like mahogany.

TWO

CONIFEROUS FATHERS

Let's fashion gentle fathers, expressive—holding us
how we wanted to be held before we could ask.

Singing off-key lullabies, written for us—songs
every evening, like possibilities. Fathers who say,

This is how you hold a baby, but never mention
a football. Say nothing in that moment, just bring

us to their chests naturally, without shyness.
Let's grow fathers from pine, not oak, coniferous

fathers raising us in their shade, fathers soft enough
to bend—fathers who love us like their fathers

couldn't. Fathers who can talk about menstruation
while playing a game of pepper in the front yard.

No, take baseball out. Let's discover a new sort—
fathers as varied and vast as the Superior Forest.

Let's kill off sternness and play down wisdom;
give us fathers of laughter and fathers who cry,

fathers who say *Check this out*, *I'm scared*,
I'm sorry, or *I don't know*. Give us fathers strong enough

to admit they want to be near us; they've always
wanted to be near us. Give us fathers desperate

for something different, not Johnny Appleseed,
not even Atticus Finch. No more rolling stones.

No more La-Z-Boy dads reading newspapers in
some other room. Let's create folklore side-by-side

in a garden singing psalms about abiding—just that,
abiding: being steadfast, present, evergreen, and

ethereal—let's make the old needles soft enough
for us to rest on, dream on, next to them.

GESTATION FANTASY

This time his shoes press against her bladder.
His feet are somewhere else. She went in
to clear his closet and found him alive
there, his body-spray lingering on clothes he left
behind. She breathes his skin. His hair continues
to grow; she swears she can hear it. She rests
her head on his old wool jacket, lets his big sneakers
dig into her spine. Ambient light seeps under
the door, climbs up the wood inside.
There is a specific line where the light ends
and darkness begins. She focuses there.
She trains her eyes on that penumbra
until she floats: cells within a cell. Dreams:
the closet becomes space that nourishes—
sanctuary within darkness. A place where
she provided everything he needed to survive.
Shelter where he could thrive
while the light got ready to receive him.

ARTERIAL

Bits of genetic material and cells [pass] not only from
mother to child but also from child to mother.
—SCIENTIFIC AMERICAN, APRIL 30, 2010

&
you
were created
so you
might create
&
when
you gave life
you came
alive too
&
just as
the source
connects
to river
thru a narrow
tributary
river returns
bits of itself
back to
water
from which
it came
so if it's
drawn down
while its source
is still there
river lives

on in its
creator
  &
in this
way a bed
once
carved
ever remains
&
river
made dry
flows
on
  &

CONFLUENCE

for K.K.D.

On a weekday morning we made our way to work
as a dense fog held low against the city, clouds

descended to earth. You were on foot. Surrounded
by fox and deer you could not see. I was miles away,

crossing a bridge over the Minnesota River. Mist
gathered just above the water made me think of marriage.

I returned to a difficult day, a week before our wedding
when we went for an ultrasound. Your chatty nurse

fell quiet as she scanned your belly. We stared into
a mysterious gray. Later, you called to let me know

what we lost. We became apparitions. I came to you
and lay beside you in silence. For the first time,

I held your soft body to mine and felt sadness.
That was the day we were married. That was the day

I realized marriage expands two lives to one.
That was the day I grasped ache as hunger,

misery within desire, how our days show us many
different forms. I remembered this that foggy morning

watching water wait above water, and again today,
our other anniversary. My love, I make this to tell you—

you made me right: everything is amplified. Joy doubles,
also pain. The endless work of the river, the haze around it.

LOST IN THE CROWD

In the flatter dimension of pictures, there is length
and width but no depth. Faces speak lies. Devoid

of sound, viewed from afar, intense pain masquerades
as glee. Thoughtfulness communicates consternation.

The imperfect smile of a happy man is wariness.
A face that speaks only truth—through silence

and through noise, even to eyes that have never
encountered this countenance—is the face of

a mother who has just lost her child.
Here she is now. Her boy stopped, face down

in the middle of an American street. Look at him.
Bits of his gray, pools of his red envelop him.

Surrounding her, in the full world and the flat one,
other faces speak only truth—register her loss,

try to fathom it, fall short—faces of pity.
We gawk without shame. We give ourselves license

to stare awhile—several seconds. None of it
matters to the mother who just lost her child—

naked in her grief, molting, becoming something
else, so transformed by anguish, by terror,

she doesn't even know we're watching.

INNOCENCE AS COLLATERAL

Notice the children.
I count six. A girl, about eight,
wanders by, wonders why
the woman hurts like this.
The boys, four, on the edge
of a curb, hold hands, sway
their courage up to leap, leap—
land—just fine today. One,
a bit older, two feet too tall to be
held, holds on now for dear life
just above her belly button.
Just below her chest, life
arrived through a cord.
Life was gleaned from her
breasts. Life is of her body.
Life is her body—feeding,
receiving, clinging, cleaving,
a cleaving, a leaving, leaving.

BACK IN HUNTINGTON

In northeast Indianapolis a car collides with a fence, then
a wall. Its engine whines in reverse. A pistol reports once,

a windshield shatters. A man dies. Cars and trucks crawl
by. Loose change bounces around a pocket while an ID

is retrieved. Your name is now known but not yet spoken.
In Huntington, a hundred miles away, the volume on a TV

lowers to confirm a knock at the door. A few blocks
down, a cell phone rings continuously in the purse of

a woman, about your age, who makes sandwiches for
a national chain. In Spring Hill or Rocky Ripple, a man

throws his keys onto a kitchen table then collapses into
a nearby chair. His wife holds him to her chest, whispers

assurances not hers to make. *It was not your fault,* she says.
The day went sideways. It was him or you. In London, an intern

adds your name to a database of those who have died at
the hands of police this year. You are number 537; Joshua

Dyer, age 34, passenger in a car trying to get away.
In St. Paul, MN, a man joins those lamenting your loss.

He was about your son's age when his father was killed
by a different man in a different city with a different gun

for different reasons. He imagines your mother, sedated
now, television off, resting when she can find rest

in the same small living room where you played guitar
for her four days prior. He imagines your son's mother

still wearing her restaurant uniform kneeling down by
your boy, age five; she's trying to breathe through it

and be strong for him as she describes what cannot
be explained. The man in St. Paul imagines a point in

the distant future, back in Huntington on a pleasant
June day when your son says, *Mom, tell me about Dad,*

and his mother will stop doing whatever she is doing
to repeat her truth, and she will know it and know it.

Your father loved you a lot, she'll tell him. *He was tall and
thin and handsome. He wore his sideburns long and thick but*

*kept his hair short like yours. He had the warmest eyes, so blue,
and one eyebrow that went up high when he smiled, which he*

*did often. He loved music. He loved playing it; he listened to it
all the time. Your daddy made mistakes. We all do. But what*

happened to him was not his fault, she'll say, and by then
it will be true. *I'm pretty sure,* she'll add, because it will

matter to her to say it out loud to him every single
time, *I'm pretty sure you would have liked him too.*

MY ULTIMATE THOUGHT IS THIS

In conversation, a friend from my youth
who worked for a time as a prison guard
saw fit to say, *Michael, you don't know much—*
lots of these convicts are just feral beasts.
On hearing his words, I surrendered faith.
I wound myself up so I could pounce down
on his beliefs—pinned him down hard, showed
him my teeth, growled in his face from my
far better view (I despised him and his).
Chewing on the cheek of his claim, the next
to last thought to enter my head was this:
only a beast thinks a man is a beast.

WHAT NAME FOR THIS?

Do you hold salt—
                            or beads?
    Wood or wool?
                    Someone else's hand
        or your own?

Do you kneel?
            Lift one hand high above your head?

Or do you shine the light of your palms
                                    up toward sky?

            Do you raise your chin? Close your eyes?
                    Is light returned to you?

Do you sit on a floor, shoeless? Chant?
            Do you fold your body gently onto itself—

    shins to earth, seat to feet, chest to knees?
                    Are you among brothers or sisters?

            Are you alone sometimes?

Do you call it morning light
                            or dawn prayer?

Is it the flour offering
                    or do you ask for daily bread?

            What do you say at dusk, at night?
        And what do you seek in supplication?

What do you offer:
           water or fruit, flowers or incense?

Do you give your servant self?
           To what, may I ask? To what?

I rest my sit bones on wood and wool,
        on leather. My feet touch carpet,

    pine, metal. I make circles and lines.
Sometimes, everything reduces to circles and lines.

I call this providence—I know
           that's not the right word.

I find this at home in my kitchen
     or at my desk. Sometimes this finds me

    when I'm on a bicycle surrounded
by cars or trees, shoulders low

and curved, back arched, my chest
     deflated and down, and me

at work to keep everything round.
     Sometimes there, I hear birds

    or squirrels chant above me.
Other times, I am summoned

    to spaces magnified in community.
What name for this? I feel called.

I walk forward to say this—this is what
I have to offer: one part of my small story.

Or, this is what I've witnessed;
                I want you to notice it, too.

        My hands, my grasp,
sometimes, they only claim air. Sweet

siblings, we're here—together—either way,
        what name must we give

to this beyond our words?

~~ANOTHER BLACK~~ MAN ~~KILLED IN POLICE~~ ~~CUSTODY~~ DIES AFTER COMA

~~Baltimore, Maryland~~ Sandtown-Winchester area of West Baltimore.
Police officers ~~abused~~ apprehended
a 25-year-old black ~~man~~ male ~~named Freddie Gray~~
~~after~~ for ~~allegedly finding him in~~ possession of a ~~knife~~ switchblade.

~~The officers threw Mr. Gray into the back of a police van.~~
The officers placed the suspect into a department vehicle.
He was handcuffed at the time in keeping with standard protocol.
The officers ~~gave Mr. Gray a "rough ride,"~~
~~which is also known as a "cowboy ride" or a "nickel ride,"~~
transported the suspect to a detention facility for questioning.

~~As a result of injuries sustained in the rough ride,~~
~~Mr. Gray broke his spinal cord and severely damaged his larynx.~~
~~Police officers ignored his requests for help at least three separate times~~
~~and let him suffer without any aid.~~

Upon arrival, the officers noticed the suspect appeared to be injured.
~~Eventually,~~ Paramedics were called, and he was transported to a hospital.
~~Mr. Gray was resuscitated and underwent extensive surgery~~
~~to repair his larynx.~~ Despite ~~these~~ best efforts,

~~Mr. Gray~~ the suspect fell into a coma and died a week later
~~as a direct result of injuries sustained while in police custody.~~

Police encountered ~~Mr. Gray~~ the suspect
on the morning of April 12, 2015,
in the Sandtown-Winchester area of West Baltimore.

~~Mr. Gray~~ **Unprovoked, the suspect** attempted to flee on foot,
but police ~~chased and tackled~~ **detained** him, searched him,
found a ~~knife~~ **switchblade** in his pocket,
and took him into custody at 8:40 a.m.

~~Two bystanders captured Mr. Gray's arrest with video recordings~~
~~showing Mr. Gray being dragged into the van by officers.~~

~~A bystander who knew Mr. Gray said the officers were "folding" him.~~

~~Folding is a tactic often deployed by the Baltimore Police Department~~
~~wherein one officer bends a citizen's legs backwards~~
~~while another officer holds the citizen down~~
~~by putting a knee on his or her neck.~~

~~Another person witnessed Mr. Gray being beaten with batons.~~

~~Freddie Gray was the son of Gloria Darden.~~
~~He had a twin sister, Fredericka, and another sister, Carolina.~~

~~At the time of his death, Mr. Gray~~ **The suspect** lived
~~in a house owned by his sisters~~ in the **notorious**
Gilmor Homes neighborhood.
~~He was 5 feet 8 inches tall and weighed 145 pounds~~

The suspect was later identified as "Freddie" Gray.
~~As with many young men growing up under similar circumstances —~~
~~marginalized, disenfranchised, and unheard, Mr. Gray~~

He had a **lengthy** criminal record~~;~~
~~mainly for misdemeanors and drug-related offenses.~~

Gray had been arrested a total of 22 times in Maryland.
He had been involved in 20 criminal court cases—
five of which were still active at the time of his death.

The ~~unnamed~~ police officers ~~who killed~~
~~Mr. Gray~~ **who took Gray into custody**
are on ~~paid~~ administrative leave pending
the outcome of an ~~internal~~ investigation.

GRINDING DOWN TO PRAYER
for George Floyd

I woke to the news you were dead.
The what arrived before daylight;

the how was agony unfolding as I
dreaded my way to dusk. Unfolding

against my want not to know
(but I already knew, have known

since I could know): *officers, arrest,*
Black, man, twenty, video, knee,

sir, back, dollar, 8, counterfeit,
hands, sorry, 46, mama, please,

breathe, please! Were you tired
George? I feel tired sometimes.

America on my neck—my
lungs compressed so much

they can't expand/contract—
take in/send out—oxygen/words.

My dentist says I grind my teeth.
My molars are wearing smooth.

The next night, I jolted awake
to find my fists clenched tight

(some fight), my heart pounding fast,
my mouth hanging open, slack,

not tight that time, just me
on my own gasping for air

6 times a minute—a raspy sound.
The world was darkness; my room was

darkness. I lay in a state of
in between and thought of you

but also God. I wanted the sun
but did not ask. I hoped instead

for a quiet dawn and peace for us,
real peace for us. I hoped so hard

it almost made a prayer.

FIXTURES

Fog borne of fatigue, fog of early morning,
of restless middle-years sleeplessness, fog of cat
hair in my eye, of dog, dogs, fog of darkness, fog

of dreary days under a pseudo-autocracy, funk
fog of high crimes and misdemeanors, fog of my daily
compulsion toward work I do not want to do.

Red traffic light unaware I am there. Darkness,
no cars coming, no reason to wait—no policy
vindicated by my compliance: left, then right, then

left again. Headlights on, brake lights working,
me a warrantless man, a man without priors,
an insured man—able to prove it. No cars coming,

no reason to wait. I run it. I run it every day. I run
the red light like I'm free. In the Midwest we don't
really have bodegas. We have convenience stores

or mini-marts fueled by fuel, for cars, for people,
fuel and cigarettes, vapes, energy drinks, chips,
dips, nuts, so many kinds of cold beverage, even 3.2

beer, and there's one kind of fruit: browning bananas,
three for a buck. Sinful things: donuts, deli delights
pre-packaged off-site, pornos and pills, tinctures

and balms, ointments—get hard, stay hard, chill out,
grab a boost, fight acid, soothe your cough—fuel fix
and run. The mini-mart I go to is in the 'burbs, two

miles away from three supermarkets. It's called
Farmer's Grandson Eatery—no 2nd possessive so
it applies to me through my mother's father, but

membership bestows no advantage. I go there
because it's easy—right off the interstate. My mini-
mart makes hot sandwiches on site. I stop even

though I know my foray will be plagued by malaise.
All of us dumb from exhaustion, everything taking
too damn long, no one speaking except Ahmed,

his is the only name I know, he who credits me
for a coffee club I ain't in, waves me away like
a blessed child, recognizes me and my usual fare:

medium roast in a medium cup, always either
almost enough cream or a bit too much. Once, on
a snowy morning, I trudged to a bodega in Harlem,

144th and Amsterdam—dispatched on a parental
errand, in a hurry, urgent a.m. appointment
midtown, knowing traffic would crawl, knowing

the snow would pack the A-train, needing good
food to go, arrived to find the owner—brown
like me and tired too—out of bagels, the bakery

delayed by the storm. I said nothing. Somehow,
he knew my mission mattered. He left me by the till,
walked aisles more narrow than I, then returned

with a mango and a small plastic knife. I don't know
the name of the woman at my mini-mart who rang
me up most mornings. I don't know where she is

from—North America, South, Central. She is brown
like me and not. We've never spoken, and in my full
humanity and hers, being honest, I didn't like her

much, nor she much me, I think. All our transactions
drowned in dread. She dropped change in my hand
like I was hot. High voltage. I often wanted different

for us, though never enough to speak on it. Four
years, meeting almost every day—1,000 mornings,
sharing nothing but place. 1,000 mornings, her

presence a fixture, so familiar to me I could take
her for granted—1,000 mornings always the same:
$1.70—bag? $1.70—bag? No thank you. No thank you.

Then *no*, just *no*. Then nothing because she was
gone. She vanished or was disappeared. Though it
could have been anything, the times pushed panic.

Gone, yet she stayed with me all day—ache of
a void, wage of regret, more constant than ever;
she lingered, still with me that night as I worried

toward sleep. Darkness again the next morning
when I arrived at the red light I ran every day, still
unaware I was there. Awake, alert, clarified in concern,

chastened, willing to wait for permission to go,
reminded my compliance is the policy,
and vindication is not meant for me here, nor her.

Grace is not made for us. People so invisible
we can't see each other—hypervisible people.
People whose papers matter and don't: kin.

AMERICA IS LOVING ME TO DEATH

America is loving me to death, loving me to death slowly, and I
Mainly try not to be disappeared here, knowing she won't pledge
Even tolerance in return. Dear God I can't offer allegiance.
Right now, 400 years ago, far into the future—it's difficult to
Ignore or forgive how despised I am and have been in the
Centuries I've been here—despised in the design of the flag
And in the fealty it demands (lest I be made an example of).
In America there's one winning story—no adaptations. The
Story imagines a noble, grand progress where we're all united.
Like truths are as self-evident as the Declaration states.
Or like they would be if not for detractors like me, the ranks of
Vagabonds existing to point out what's rotten in America,
Insisting her gains come at a cost, reminding her who pays, and
Negating wild notions of exceptionalism—adding ugly facts to
God's favorite-nation mythology. Look, victors get spoils; I know the
Memories of the vanquished fade away. I hear the enduring republic,
Erect and proud, asking through ravenous teeth, *Who do you riot for?*
Tamir? Sandra? Medgar? George? Breonna? Elijah? Philando? Eric? Which
One? Like it can't be all of them. Like it can't be the entirety of it:
Destroyed brown bodies, dismantled homes, so demolition stands
Even as my fidelity falls, as it must. She erases my reason too, allows one
Answer to her only loyalty test: *Yes or no, Michael, do you love this nation?*
Then hates me for saying I can't, for not burying myself under
Her fables where we're one, indivisible, free, just, under God, her God.

THREE

ARS POETICA

In a recent dream, I wanted something ordinary—eggs
or a hammer, a thing like that. So, I sought out a neighbor

but not a real neighbor. I rang an unfamiliar bell.
Behind a hollow door, a man yelled, *I called the police.*

Okay, I said. *Do you mind if I wait for them
here?* He must have said *no* 'cause I waited on

his front steps. Soon, he sat next to me. We talked, but
I don't know what we talked about. We were calm.

I know we were calm. Neighbors chatting while sirens
gathered in volume, urgency. I never got the ordinary

thing. Worse, I woke myself up seconds before the police
arrived to arrest me. The squad car and its lights disappeared.

I usually return to darkness—my dreams gone, lost,
beyond my reach, into my cortex, into ether. Or maybe

that's what I tell myself. It's possible I don't want to know
what my mind makes when I sleep. I may rely on forgetting.

I'm writing this on my phone while I teach my daughter to drive.
I should pay attention more than I do, but she is managing well,

and I don't want to lose this idea. *I'm writing a poem*, I tell her.
She asks, *What about?* I answer. *Cool,* she says. I say, *I almost*

*always forget my dreams I don't know why. Maybe I want more
from them—like magic—something fantastic. Maybe*

I could breathe underwater or be miniscule or grow an epic beard
or maybe all three at the same time. Sadly, my vision is common.

I dream about ordinary things—stuff that could actually happen.
As I say this, my daughter sits like a dancer, tall and open.

Her hands show power and lightness. In them,
the steering wheel becomes a ballet barre.

She's focused, but she is somewhere else too.
I always remember my dreams, she says. *They're strange.*

In one, I pooped a yellow snake then became friends with it.
Are you shitting me? I ask. She frowns, shifts gears,

rolls her eyes, shakes her head, and she's right. This
is a serious conversation. Time is silent. We practice

turns, left and right. We do road work. I navigate.
We avoid busy streets. We'll work our way up to them.

I reach a spot where I can stop writing the poem.
Quiet becomes a taunt, a gauntlet. Eventually, I say,

You are the kind of artist I want to be. She does
not look at me. She keeps her eyes on the road. She makes

the window a mirror, meets me there instead.

POSTCARD FROM THE BOTTOM OF A LAKE
for A.L.

In Maiden Rock, along Pepin's north shore,
a single hawk hovers in late-morning sky—swift
shadow across pale blue white. Its glide suggests
effortlessness. Summer now and nestlings can fly.
I'm on retreat seeking lightness and quiet. Here, inside
a cottage surrounded by windows through which
I see day lilies and trees, butterflies and passerines.
In my writer's thesaurus, 'diurnal' follows 'ditzy'
and ditzy means 'featherbrained,' and this proximity
to the word I sought feels serendipitous. Did you know
Lake Pepin exists in two states? At dusk, I'll swim
there and watch ruthless birds ride the thermals—
parents free of offspring, juveniles migrating away.
I'll float—imagining my fledgling fledged, myself
fledged. Later when my work is done, I will
dive into the vast lake sourced by a river
that is always, always flowing south.

WORLDLY THINGS

large clay pot   ancestral
seeds   an old hand
mill to grind
my yield a little salt
my body bent to knead
this oven

two batteries one bulb
ore and blasting   heat wires
casting molds I've made
a switch

a knife   one roll
of tape   an empty
oatmeal can   sand
paper photo paper
the finest I can find
a patch of foil on which
I'll press a sharp pin
down to make   a tiny hole
darkness sufficient
exposure to light

these things I bring
to my writing desk
workshop inside
my kitchen this room
where I sweat bake
dense food   pattern
light beams snap-
shots craft
images and other devices
meant to survive   me

HERE ALL ALONE

Raptors ride the thermals above Dakota.
Beyond them, the sun appears closer,
colder. Everything warm escapes, returns.
One hundred nations assemble in congress,
this time for water, where water is life.
And I know this isn't my song to sing,

but I wonder what god saves grace for hunters.

Water cannons, fire hoses, *nunc pro tunc.*
This land, once yours, was flooded and dammed
the same day our Rondo was cleaved for a highway.
And I know I've seen those attack dogs before
with the same blue force undoing brown bodies.
Foul water in Flint, good water in Bismarck:
bullets, bulldozers, bad pipes, hollow promises—
what birds are these still circling, circling

while god denies grace for the hunted?

Warm air sent rising makes gliding
look easy, while shale beneath us fractures,
relents. So why must earth grow colder then
harden, and leave us to shiver here all alone,
singing sad songs of foremothers, forefathers
while above the raptors exhort us to prey?

To pray to a god who saves grace for hunters.

ACCESS

For every disruption, corresponding
devastations, every fallen figure topples
all the tiles around it.

this is what she was wearing when
she was interrupted this is what she did
what she said how her face was

unmade her chest unbounded in
its grief bear witness now bear witness
while her eyes dance then depart

Intimate moments seldom witnessed
before, though they occurred
often. Until we downloaded

omniscience, they didn't exist
really. We just pretended
we didn't know.

POSTCARD TO SEAN
for S.H.

or fraternity or chance. For example, I might write
I thought of you the other day on a trail through woods
due south of the Minnesota River, just west of the capitol.
So quiet there I heard critters scurry along the path and leaves
and twigs rustle and snap—my own feet falling while I puzzled
my way through some particular poem part, wanting to know
more about prayer, a specific Catholic prayer I used to recite.
Sean, a bird tweeted or trilled a morning song quite short,
quite grand. It got me wondering what creature calls with notes
above the rattle? Which led me back to you who might know
or research until you did, you out west in Fairbanks, north of me
yet, still sleeping, or up with your baby boy as once I was up
with my baby girl. Or I might write to fatherhood instead
or happenstance. Because postcards to people are postcards
to ideas to ideals to abstractions; they're psalms, quite short.
Anyway, I wanted to reach out to you and these other things to say,
brother, I looked it up. I'm pretty sure it was an indigo bunting.

PRESTIDIGITATION

On a day too hot for clouds, wind, or eight-year-olds,
our grandfather took my brother and me fishing

at an overstocked pond just outside Wichita.
We rode in a row in his green and white Chevy truck—

three on the tree. Our dad was gone now, unmade
instantly by a man with his finger on a trigger.

Grandfather was knighted our surrogate. I remember
his massive hands, so sure at the wheel, each round

knuckle witness to his life of labor. My grandfather's
name was Arthur, and he talked all the time about

his arthritis but pronounced it *autha-itis*, so for months
I thought it was a condition unique to him, that he

had his own special burden, just like my brother
and me. I remember the truck's cabin engulfed by

his musk: his aftershave with hints of cedarwood
and tonka, his brandy breath, Prince Albert fuming

perpetually from his pipe. Eventually, we arrived at
a catfish farm, shadeless and stark. We walked to

a shed and found a man about my grandfather's age,
his face red like a traffic light. We bought bait and

tackle and showed our backs to the sun. We set
our hooks and casted our lines, casted our lines.

In time, I landed one. Your reel motion stops when
you catch on a catfish. You think you're snagged.

The fish was bigger than I imagined and stronger.
I brought it in on my own but couldn't get my small

hands on it. I was afraid. So, I watched grandfather
disregard its barbels and free it from the hook

with casual ease, his hands calloused and rough,
impervious to whips and stings. I understood

someday I would need to be like that too. Between
the three of us we caught eight fish that day—eight

good catfish. We were there an hour or two. Brother
and I knew enough not to complain about the heat,

but this was an early lesson and this was time
for grace. When we were done, we gathered our things

to head to our grandparents' house, to head back
home. We took our catch in an old gray bucket

back to the shed to pay. We poured them into a metal pan
spotted with rust, rectangular and shallow. I watched

as the catfish fought and thrashed wildly, worked for
the surface, took in hot air with their mouths, beat

frantically against each other and the pan until the old
man in the shed flipped a light switch on then off. It was

up on the wall five feet or so, connected to the pan
by a wire-mold raceway. I hadn't noticed the setup

before he reached over to it, but even now I
remember how nonchalant that man was,

how suddenly the fish stopped moving at all,
how still they were, how calm.

ADORATION

Light pans my dark
bedroom like a copier

scans an image. My
father floats by me

sometimes. He was
called James or Jim.

His mustache stayed
neat and mean; he

groomed it every day.
My father adored

suits and ties. At home,
top button unbuttoned,

he smelled often of
aftershave and whiskey.

He is gone. He is
gone now. Still,

forty years later,
I taste his shadow

and balm on my lips
from the last time

I kissed his
sandpaper face

good morning.

EMBOUCHURE

I don't know how trumpets work. This wondering woke me
into a Saturday with my beloved beside me as she has been
for more than a third of my days, a being, asleep so only
her head and hair are visible, a wonder I might understand,
if understanding was possible. I know there are three buttons,
I know you can push one of them or any two or none or all.
I know when you breathe into it, the horn can make a lot
of different notes, so everything else must happen through
the lips, the tongue, the lungs, the diaphragm, the body.

STRUCTURAL FATIGUE

A band I love released
another album. I watch them
on YouTube while walking my dog.

My neighbor Bob appears ashen
in a second-floor window
framed in waning yellow light.

Just home from work, I walk
our Goldendoodle in darkness.
Streetlights make skinny shadows of us.

In the video the band looks haggard,
older, strung out maybe. They
mock earlier versions of themselves.

Bob and I had a competition
for best shovel and best mow, except
he had no idea we were competing.

Buds in, volume up, senses down.
These are safe streets, but I can't see
much or hear outside of the song.

The boys in the band are
half my age; they live and describe
a zeitgeist different than mine.

Months ago, Bob, already frail, at least
an octogenarian, suddenly stopped
mowing or shoveling. He vanished.

Puppy and I reach a dark house where
a shy woman lives with a chatty man.
Their Pomeranian is barkless and old.

The band has an esoteric name,
unrelated to anything really, three words:
one syllable, one syllable, two.

Barb took over. She's tiny, lovely, married
to Bob. Now she shovels and mows
and plucks creeping charlie by hand.

My puppy is eight months and chaos.
The Pomeranian sits in an unlit yard—doesn't
know we're coming 'til we're already there.

The band sings about sex and alcohol
and mortality. Their song includes one
of those direct-address meta-moments.

I hadn't seen Bob in many months
when he appeared, small in his window,
staring at nothing—petrified.

In my ear then, the band asked,
*...dooon't you re-a-lize our bo-dies
could fall a-part at a-ny se-cond?*

Here's the deal: structural fatigue
eventually causes breakdowns. I am 50
and chaos. My whole body groans.

Never have I ever shoveled or mowed
better than Bob or Barb. Doesn't matter
anyway—very little does. Watching Bob

in his window, I notice for the first time
the complex time signatures—all
the instruments play a different meter.

I imagine myself decades hence, which is
selfish, I know, but I am somewhere
inside the middle of my life, and still

preoccupied with sex, alcohol, and
mortality—only the ratios have changed.
I write to you 500 days into a desperate reign,

alchemy is over-subscribed.
People line up for more. I'm wide-eyed
and tired, but last night I had a dream

and in the dream I was asleep. I needed
more rest. I tried to wake in the dream
without waking myself up in real life.

It can't be done. We arrive
to a lightless place; our shadows
disappear but remain.

The song is about the song,
and I can't deny I am enervated.
Our king is mad. Our king is grim,

dim, dimming. Our king is mean.
The boys in the band convert fragility
to urgency—they want to get laid.

Bob waits to stop waiting, whitened
down to gray, to blue—quiet
as an empty house, a sleepy reverie,

and I know he has forgotten me.
At last, I answer them and him, no one,
everyone—*I do*, I say it out loud—*I do. I do.*

DISPATCH FROM MIDDLE AMERICA
for Murray Middle School

The Karen are here and the Hmong. Ethiopians, Eritreans, and the Somali are here. They are here from Europe, Mexico, and Canada. Americans are here, first generation and seventh generation and Indigenous. Black and white, Asian—every race and ethnicity—they are all here. Christians and Jews, Muslims and Hindus, Buddhists and UUs and atheists, so many faiths are here. A single Rastafarian is here. He's white, his colorful clothes always adorned with the leaf of his sacred herb. He walks among girls in abaya or chador, hijab, dupatta. The comically tall and the very short. The wealthy and the poor. Children of the hyper-educated, children of the semi-literate, broken children and blessed children. Here. Gay boys are here. Lesbians and bisexuals, trans and queer kids are here. They are all here. Each of them and all of them. Here with their dreams and desires, their dramas and disturbances. Some flowers blossoming in radiant display, some seeds wanting water and fertile soil. But here. They laugh, and they cry. Some hit each other, some fuck each other. Some try smoking or drinking or pills or love. But they all bounce about here, for your consideration, perpetually in flux at a single middle-school in Saint Paul, in Minnesota, in the Upper-Midwest of America. Half asleep and completely alive with their phones and their ear buds, their affectations and their urgency—all as if to say: look at me. Please don't look at me. Help me. Please leave me alone. Go away please. Never leave me. Here, please. Here.

DORMANCY

for Grace Glass (February 11, 1916 – November 11, 2013)

sometimes in winter I imagine
a November afternoon

green leaves unfurl on trees underground
as we bury my grandmother next to her husband

everything's inverted
at a cemetery in Wichita, Kansas

what shoots above are roots
we place her in the ground like a seed in a hull

we know from science this doesn't happen
after a vibrant autumn

trees enter dormancy
night grows darker, colder

leaves fall off, change slows
but instead of decaying, she germinates—

THE GROVE

Planted here as we are, see how we want
to bow and sway with the motion of earth
in sky. Feel how desire vibrates within us
as our branches fan out, promise entanglements,
rarely touch. Here, our sweet rustlings. If only
we could know how twisted up our roots
are, we might make vast shelter together—
cooler places, verdant spaces, more sustaining
air. But we are strange trees, reluctant in this
forest—we oak and ash, we pine—
the same the same, not different. All of us
reach toward star and cloud, all of us want
our share of light, just enough rainfall.

EVERY MOURNING

Morning: walking my neighborhood, I come upon a colony
of ants busy at work. I take care not to step on any and miss

them all, then encounter up a ways a fellow traveler greeting
the day. I am frightening her. No. She is afraid of me.

Is she an introvert? Is she a neighbor? Is she just in from the 'burbs,
from the country? Is she scared of the inner city? Am I the inner city?

Is she racist? Shouldn't I be the wary one? Or is she a survivor
like me? It can't be what I'm wearing: khakis, a blue and white

checkered button-down shirt, and the nylon sandals I favor
because they're comfortable, my feet can breathe in them.

Dear friends, I am the nicest man on earth.

And I want to shout, *Morning!* But just then a weaver or
carpenter, just then a pharaoh or fire or pavement, just

then a little black ant struggles by alone, alone. And
in that moment, I want us to give ourselves over

to industry, carry the weight of the day together, lighten
it. I want to be a part of a colony where I feel easy

walking around. Cool as the goddamn breeze. Where
I can breathe, build structures sturdier and grander

than this—but the woman crosses to the other side
of the street, and I do what I usually do: retreat into

myself as far as I can, then send out whatever's left.

NOTES

"Access," "Arterial," "Gestation Fantasy," "Innocence as Collateral," and "Lost in the Crowd" were inspired by a YouTube video of a mother who just learned her child was killed by police.

"Structural Fatigue" references the song "Bodys" by Car Seat Headrest.

"Man Dies After Coma" imagines a newspaper articles written in plain text, then edited by an editor who deleted some language, using strikethrough, and added new language, using bold text. The poem was assembled using information obtained from multiple newspaper articles and online sources.

"America is Loving Me to Death" is an acrostic golden shovel, the merger of two forms. The first letter in each line makes the poem acrostic and, when read down, spells the phrase, *America is loving me to death.* In golden shovels, the last word in each line is a quote, often from a poem or song. In this case, the quote is the first twenty-four words of the Pledge of Allegiance.

My sincere gratitude to each of the publications where the following poems first appeared:

"Every Mourning," "My Ultimate Thought Is This," and "Dispatch from Middle America," *Potomac Review*, Issue 68, Spring 2021

"Grinding Down to Prayer" first appeared as "Apnea & Bruxism" in the chapbook *Can't Stop Won't Stop, Rain Taxi Review*, January 2021

"Prestidigitation" and "After they left," *Poetry Northwest*, Winter and Spring 2021

"Gloria Mundi" *Memorious*, Issue 31, December 2020

"America Is Loving Me to Death," Poem-a-Day, Poets.Org, November 2020

"Here All Alone" and "Structural Fatigue," *Midway Journal*, Vol. 13, Issue 3

"Coniferous Fathers" first appeared in *Poetry of Resistance and Change*, Sister Black Press, 2017

"Coniferous Fathers" also appeared in *The Road by Heart: Poems of Fatherhood*, Greg Watson, Editor, Nodin Press, Spring 2018

"Coniferous Fathers" was also included in *Stone Gathering*, Fall 2019

"Ars Poetica," was also included in *The Road by Heart: Poems of Fatherhood*, Greg Watson, Editor, Nodin Press, Spring 2018

"Ode to My Mother's Face" and "A Simple Question," *Poetry City*, Winter 2018

"Embouchure" and "Postcard to Anne," *North Dakota Quarterly*, Winter 2018

"Seismic Activities," "Man Dies After Coma," "Confluence," "Superman and My Brother, Spiderman and Me," and "End of Class," *Sleet Magazine,* Spring/Summer 2021

ACKNOWLEDGMENTS

To my family, including the family I gained by marriage—thank you.

Juliet Patterson helped me see myself as a poet. So much of what I've learned about poetry, I've learned from her. Juliet is an exemplary teacher, a brilliant and beautiful writer, and a dear friend.

My mom, Lequetta Diggs, told me many, many times "you can do anything you put your mind to." She said it with unwavering conviction, and, even as I can list hundreds of things I cannot do, sometimes I believe in myself in spite of myself because my entire life I've had someone who believes in me.

Karen Kleber Diggs has been tireless in her support of my writing. To the extent I have space to write and edit, arrange and rearrange, fidget and dream, I have it because of Karen. Thank you my love.

I learn a lot about art and creativity from my daughter, Elinor Kleber Diggs. Her ability to embrace and shape ideas that come to her are an inspiration to me. She is "the kind of artist I want to be."

I feel the same way about my twin brother, Martin Diggs. His drawing, painting, and photography have been an inspiration to me for as long as I can remember.

Thank you to Gabriella Anaïs Deal-Márquez, whose insights and ideas, encouragement and "accountability sessions" have inspired me to work harder, go deeper within my work, and dream plans into action.

I had a life-changing visit with Su Hwang and Sun Yung Shin on a warm spring day in San Antonio, Texas. On the spot, I sent a draft of my manuscript to Su for feedback. Her ideas helped me see my stack of poems as a cohesive book. Beyond the priceless gift of her ideas, Su encourages me in ways too numerous to count. Thank you.

My sincere gratitude and appreciation to Henri Cole who selected *Worldly Things* for the Max Ritvo Poetry Prize and to Dr. Riva Ariella Ritvo-Slifka and everyone at the Alan B. Slifka Foundation for funding the Max Ritvo Poetry Prize and supporting emerging poets.

Thanks also to Hadara Bar-Nadav. I am grateful to you for your thoughtfulness, care, and encouragement.

I owe a debt of gratitude to the writers below, dear friends, who shared feedback on the poems in this collection. Included among them are Romelle Adkins, Maya Beck, Lisa Marie Brimmer, Marisha Chamberlain, Stephanie Chrismon, Paula Cisewski, Charlie Curry, Heidi Czerwiec, Cherish Sonja Gibson, Isela Xitlali Gomez, Sean Hill, Carolyn Holbrook, Lissa Horneber, Heidi Howell Farrah, Irna Landrum, Haley Lasché, Joi Lewis, Jodi Lulich, Jeanne Lutz, Matt Mauch, Beth Mayer, Jill Mazullo, Lynda McDonnell, Mary Moore Easter, Kara Olson, Timothy Otte, Juliet Patterson, Kasey Payette, Sherri Quan Lee, Glenda Reed, Katie Robinson, Karen Schultz, Sagirah Shahid, James Bernard Short, Penelope Simison, Danez Smith, Mike Staeger, James Stephenson, Elizabeth Tannen, Lee Colin Thomas, Kay Welsch, and Carolyn Williams-Noren.

I've learned a great deal from the students, mentors, and instructors I work with through the Minnesota Prison Writing Workshop. Although I cannot name my students here, I am grateful for the time I've shared and the things I've learned with each of them. Thank you.

Thanks also to dear friends who support me generally, but also my writing: Heather Belgum, Rolf Belgum, Florence Brammer, Richard Brown, Nichole

Burgess, Mahadev Dovre-Wudali, Monica Edwards-Larson, Gavin Fritton, Dori Henderson, Laurie Hertzel, Alison Hiltner, Gregory Jackson, Henry Jackson, Brian Kind, Renee Ladd, Patrick Lane, Megan Mayer, Carolyn Payne, Jonathan Plummer, and Christopher Selleck.

Two of my high school English teachers helped shape me as a writer--thank you Claudia Jimenez and Martin Umansky.

I am part of the best writing community in the world, and so much of my inspiration comes from my friends, all of whom are beautiful people and talented writers. Thank you: Michael Alberti, D. Allen, Mary Austin Speaker, David Bayliss, Michael Bazzett, Jennifer Bowen, Anders Carlson Wee, Jiordan Castle, Anthony Ceballos, Sharon Chmielarz, P. Scott Cunningham, Venus DeMars, Sara Dovre-Wudali, Mark Ehling, Heid Erdrich, Sherri Fernandez-Williams, Marion Gomez, Roy Guzmán, Kate Hanson Foster, Angela Hume, Ibrahim Kaba, Megan Kaminski, Athena Kildegaard, Stanley Kusunoki, Kathryn Kysar, Ed Bok Lee, Su Love, Greg Luce, Chris Martin, Janaya Martin, Lara Mimosa Montes, Hieu Minh Nyugen, G.E. Patterson, Junauda Petrus-Nasah, Bao Phi, Matt Rasmussen, Aegor Ray, Lynette Reini-Grandell, Sun Yung Shin, Jeffrey Skemp, Hawona Sullivan Janzen, Jordan Thomas, Michael Torres, Katrina Vandenberg, Greg Watson, Ben Weaver, Clarence White, and Chavonn Williams Shen.

And, to the always on point team at Milkweed—Bailey, Claire, Daniel, Lee, Mary, Shannon, and Yanna—thank you.

MICHAEL KLEBER-DIGGS was born and raised in Kansas and now lives in St. Paul, Minnesota. His work has appeared in *Potomac Review*, *Poetry Northwest*, *Lit Hub*, *The Rumpus*, *Rain Taxi*, *McSweeney's Internet Tendency*, *Water~Stone Review*, *Midway Review*, *North Dakota Quarterly*, and a few anthologies. Michael teaches poetry and creative non-fiction through the Minnesota Prison Writers Workshop.

The fourth award of the
MAX RITVO POETRY PRIZE
is presented to
MICHAEL KLEBER-DIGGS
by
MILKWEED EDITIONS
and
THE ALAN B. SLIFKA FOUNDATION

Designed to honor the legacy of one of the most original poets to debut in recent years—and to reward outstanding poets for years to come—the Max Ritvo Poetry Prize awards $10,000 and publication by Milkweed Editions to the author of a debut collection of poems. The 2020 Max Ritvo Poetry Prize was judged by Henri Cole.

Milkweed Editions thanks the Alan B. Slifka Foundation and its president, Riva Ariella Ritvo-Slifka, for supporting the Max Ritvo Poetry Prize.

milkweed
editions

Founded as a nonprofit organization in 1980, Milkweed Editions is an independent publisher. Our mission is to identify, nurture and publish transformative literature, and build an engaged community around it.

Milkweed Editions is based in Bdé Óta Othúŋwe (Minneapolis) within Mní Sota Makhóčhe, the traditional homeland of the Dakhóta people. Residing here since time immemorial, Dakhóta people still call Mní Sota Makhóčhe home, with four federally recognized Dakhóta nations and many more Dakhóta people residing in what is now the state of Minnesota. Due to continued legacies of colonization, genocide, and forced removal, generations of Dakhóta people remain disenfranchised from their traditional homeland. Presently, Mní Sota Makhóčhe has become a refuge and home for many Indigenous nations and peoples, including seven federally recognized Ojibwe nations. We humbly encourage our readers to reflect upon the historical legacies held in the lands they occupy.

milkweed.org

Interior design by Mary Austin Speaker
Typset in Garamond by Tijqua Daiker

Adobe Garamond is based upon the typefaces first created by Parisian printer Claude Garamond in the sixteenth century. Garamond based his typeface on the handwriting of Angelo Vergecio, librarian to King Francis I. The font's slenderness makes it one of the most eco-friendly typefaces available because it uses less ink than similar faces. Robert Slimbach created a digital version of Garamond for Adobe in 1989 and his font has become one of the most widely used typefaces in print.